# Address Book
## for the
# Twenty-First Century

Frank Stephenson
and Eileen Hargaden

**Home computer 1** _____

    **Password:**    _____ _____

                          _____ _____


**Home computer 2** _____

    **Password:**    _____ _____

                          _____ _____


**Smart Phone 1**    _____

    **Password:**    _____ _____

                          _____ _____


**Smart Phone 2**    _____

    **Password:**    _____ _____

                          _____ _____


**WiFi**

    **Password:**    _____

**A**

Business

Contact/Customer Service

_____                    _____

Web Address

_____

Log in/username        Password

_____  _____  _____  _____  _____

_____  _____  _____  _____  _____

_____  _____  _____  _____  _____

_____  _____  _____  _____  _____

Security Question                    Answer

_____            _____

_____            _____

_____            _____

_____            _____

Business                            Contact/Customer Service

_____                    _____

Web Address

_____

Log in/username        Password

_____  _____  _____  _____  _____

_____  _____  _____  _____  _____

_____  _____  _____  _____  _____

_____  _____  _____  _____  _____

Security Question                    Answer

_____            _____

_____            _____

_____            _____

_____            _____

**Businesses and Websites**

**A**

**Business**                    **Contact/Customer Service**

_____    _____

**Web Address**

_____

**Log in/username**    **Password**

_____  _____  _____  _____  _____

_____  _____  _____  _____  _____

_____  _____  _____  _____  _____

_____  _____  _____  _____  _____

**Security Question**              **Answer**

_____        _____

_____        _____

_____        _____

_____        _____

**Business**                    **Contact/Customer Service**

_____    _____

**Web Address**

_____

**Log in/username**    **Password**

_____  _____  _____  _____  _____

_____  _____  _____  _____  _____

_____  _____  _____  _____  _____

_____  _____  _____  _____  _____

**Security Question**              **Answer**

_____        _____

_____        _____

_____        _____

_____        _____

**Businesses and Websites**

# A

**Business**                     **Contact/Customer Service**

_____          _____

**Web Address**

_____

**Log in/username**      **Password**

_____  _____  _____  _____  _____
_____  _____  _____  _____  _____
_____  _____  _____  _____  _____
_____  _____  _____  _____  _____

**Security Question**            **Answer**

_____             _____
_____             _____
_____             _____
_____             _____

---

**Business**                     **Contact/Customer Service**

_____          _____

**Web Address**

_____

**Log in/username**      **Password**

_____  _____  _____  _____  _____
_____  _____  _____  _____  _____
_____  _____  _____  _____  _____
_____  _____  _____  _____  _____

**Security Question**            **Answer**

_____             _____
_____             _____
_____             _____
_____             _____

**Business**                    **Contact/Customer Service**
_____             _____

**Web Address**
_____

**Log in/username**    **Password**
_____  _____  _____  _____  _____
_____  _____  _____  _____  _____
_____  _____  _____  _____  _____
_____  _____  _____  _____  _____

**Security Question**           **Answer**
_____             _____
_____             _____
_____             _____
_____             _____

**Business**                    **Contact/Customer Service**
_____             _____

**Web Address**
_____

**Log in/username**    **Password**
_____  _____  _____  _____  _____
_____  _____  _____  _____  _____
_____  _____  _____  _____  _____
_____  _____  _____  _____  _____

**Security Question**           **Answer**
_____             _____
_____             _____
_____             _____
_____             _____

**Businesses and Websites**

**B**

**Businesses and Websites**

**Business**                    **Contact/Customer Service**
_____    _____

**Web Address**
_____

**Log in/username**    **Password**
_____  _____  _____  _____  _____
_____  _____  _____  _____  _____
_____  _____  _____  _____  _____
_____  _____  _____  _____  _____

**Security Question**            **Answer**
_____         _____
_____         _____
_____         _____
_____         _____

**Business**                    **Contact/Customer Service**
_____    _____

**Web Address**
_____

**Log in/username**    **Password**
_____  _____  _____  _____  _____
_____  _____  _____  _____  _____
_____  _____  _____  _____  _____
_____  _____  _____  _____  _____

**Security Question**            **Answer**
_____         _____
_____         _____
_____         _____
_____         _____

**Business**                          **Contact/Customer Service**

_____        _____

**Web Address**

_____

**Log in/username**        **Password**

_____  _____  _____  _____  _____

_____  _____  _____  _____  _____

_____  _____  _____  _____  _____

_____  _____  _____  _____  _____

**Security Question**                **Answer**

_____        _____

_____        _____

_____        _____

_____        _____

---

**Business**                          **Contact/Customer Service**

_____        _____

**Web Address**

_____

**Log in/username**        **Password**

_____  _____  _____  _____  _____

_____  _____  _____  _____  _____

_____  _____  _____  _____  _____

_____  _____  _____  _____  _____

**Security Question**                **Answer**

_____        _____

_____        _____

_____        _____

_____        _____

**B**

Business      Contact/Customer Service

_____ _____

Web Address

_____

Log in/username  Password

_____ _____ _____ _____ _____

_____ _____ _____ _____ _____

_____ _____ _____ _____ _____

_____ _____ _____ _____ _____

Security Question    Answer

_____  _____

_____  _____

_____  _____

_____  _____

Business      Contact/Customer Service

_____ _____

Web Address

_____

Log in/username  Password

_____ _____ _____ _____ _____

_____ _____ _____ _____ _____

_____ _____ _____ _____ _____

_____ _____ _____ _____ _____

Security Question    Answer

_____  _____

_____  _____

_____  _____

_____  _____

**Businesses and Websites**

**Business** _____ **Contact/Customer Service** _____

**Web Address** _____

**Log in/username** _____ **Password** _____ _____ _____ _____

_____ _____ _____ _____ _____

_____ _____ _____ _____ _____

_____ _____ _____ _____ _____

**Security Question**

_____

_____

_____

_____

**Answer**

_____

_____

_____

_____

**B**

**Business** _____ **Contact/Customer Service** _____

**Web Address** _____

**Log in/username** _____ **Password** _____ _____ _____ _____

_____ _____ _____ _____ _____

_____ _____ _____ _____ _____

_____ _____ _____ _____ _____

**Security Question**

_____

_____

_____

_____

**Answer**

_____

_____

_____

_____

**Businesses and Websites**

**Business**          **Contact/Customer Service**

_____    _____

**Web Address**

_____

**Log in/username**      **Password**

_____   ___   ___   ___   ___

_____   ___   ___   ___   ___

_____   ___   ___   ___   ___

_____   ___   ___   ___   ___

**Security Question**        **Answer**

_____    _____

_____    _____

_____    _____

_____    _____

**Business**          **Contact/Customer Service**

_____    _____

**Web Address**

_____

**Log in/username**      **Password**

_____   ___   ___   ___   ___

_____   ___   ___   ___   ___

_____   ___   ___   ___   ___

_____   ___   ___   ___   ___

**Security Question**        **Answer**

_____    _____

_____    _____

_____    _____

_____    _____

**Businesses and Websites**

**Business**                    **Contact/Customer Service**

_____        _____

**Web Address**

_____

**Log in/username**      **Password**

_____  _____  _____  _____  _____

_____  _____  _____  _____  _____

_____  _____  _____  _____  _____

_____  _____  _____  _____  _____

**Security Question**            **Answer**

_____        _____

_____        _____

_____        _____

_____        _____

**Business**                    **Contact/Customer Service**

_____        _____

**Web Address**

_____

**Log in/username**      **Password**

_____  _____  _____  _____  _____

_____  _____  _____  _____  _____

_____  _____  _____  _____  _____

_____  _____  _____  _____  _____

**Security Question**            **Answer**

_____        _____

_____        _____

_____        _____

_____        _____

**Businesses and Websites**

**Business**                    **Contact/Customer Service**

_____         _____

**Web Address**

_____

**Log in/username**      **Password**

_____  _____  _____  _____  _____

_____  _____  _____  _____  _____

_____  _____  _____  _____  _____

_____  _____  _____  _____  _____

**Security Question**           **Answer**

_____         _____

_____         _____

_____         _____

_____         _____

**Business**                    **Contact/Customer Service**

_____         _____

**Web Address**

_____

**Log in/username**      **Password**

_____  _____  _____  _____  _____

_____  _____  _____  _____  _____

_____  _____  _____  _____  _____

_____  _____  _____  _____  _____

**Security Question**           **Answer**

_____         _____

_____         _____

_____         _____

_____         _____

**Business** _____ **Contact/Customer Service** _____

**Web Address** _____

**Log in/username**          **Password**

_____  _____  _____  _____  _____
_____  _____  _____  _____  _____
_____  _____  _____  _____  _____
_____  _____  _____  _____  _____

**Security Question**          **Answer**

_____          _____
_____          _____
_____          _____
_____          _____

---

**Business** _____ **Contact/Customer Service** _____

**Web Address** _____

**Log in/username**          **Password**

_____  _____  _____  _____  _____
_____  _____  _____  _____  _____
_____  _____  _____  _____  _____
_____  _____  _____  _____  _____

**Security Question**          **Answer**

_____          _____
_____          _____
_____          _____
_____          _____

Businesses and Websites

Business       Contact/Customer Service

_____ _____

Web Address

**D**

_____

Log in/username  Password

_____ _____ _____ _____

_____ _____ _____ _____

_____ _____ _____ _____

_____ _____ _____ _____

Security Question   Answer

_____ _____

_____ _____

_____ _____

_____ _____

Business       Contact/Customer Service

_____ _____

Web Address

_____

Log in/username  Password

_____ _____ _____ _____

_____ _____ _____ _____

_____ _____ _____ _____

_____ _____ _____ _____

Security Question   Answer

_____ _____

_____ _____

_____ _____

_____ _____

**Businesses and Websites**

**Business** _____ **Contact/Customer Service** _____

**Web Address** _____

**Log in/username** _____ **Password** _____ _____ _____ _____

_____ _____ _____ _____ _____

_____ _____ _____ _____ _____

_____ _____ _____ _____ _____

**Security Question** **Answer**

_____ _____

_____ _____

_____ _____

_____ _____

---

**Business** _____ **Contact/Customer Service** _____

**Web Address** _____

**Log in/username** _____ **Password** _____ _____ _____ _____

_____ _____ _____ _____ _____

_____ _____ _____ _____ _____

_____ _____ _____ _____ _____

**Security Question** **Answer**

_____ _____

_____ _____

_____ _____

_____ _____

D

Businesses and Websites

15

**Business**                     **Contact/Customer Service**

_____          _____

**Web Address**

_____

**Log in/username**    **Password**

_____  _____  _____  _____  _____

_____  _____  _____  _____  _____

_____  _____  _____  _____  _____

_____  _____  _____  _____  _____

**Security Question**            **Answer**

_____          _____

_____          _____

_____          _____

_____          _____

**Business**                     **Contact/Customer Service**

_____          _____

**Web Address**

_____

**Log in/username**    **Password**

_____  _____  _____  _____  _____

_____  _____  _____  _____  _____

_____  _____  _____  _____  _____

_____  _____  _____  _____  _____

**Security Question**            **Answer**

_____          _____

_____          _____

_____          _____

_____          _____

**Businesses and Websites**

**Business** _____ **Contact/Customer Service**

_____ _____

**Web Address**

_____

**Log in/username**     **Password**

_____   _____   _____   _____   _____

_____   _____   _____   _____   _____

_____   _____   _____   _____   _____

_____   _____   _____   _____   _____

**Security Question**      **Answer**

_____     _____

_____     _____

_____     _____

_____     _____

**D**

**Business** _____ **Contact/Customer Service**

_____ _____

**Web Address**

_____

**Log in/username**     **Password**

_____   _____   _____   _____   _____

_____   _____   _____   _____   _____

_____   _____   _____   _____   _____

_____   _____   _____   _____   _____

**Security Question**      **Answer**

_____     _____

_____     _____

_____     _____

_____     _____

**Businesses and Websites**

**Business**                    **Contact/Customer Service**

_____        _____

**Web Address**

_____

**Log in/username**    **Password**

_____  _____   _____  _____  _____

_____  _____   _____  _____  _____

_____  _____   _____  _____  _____

_____  _____   _____  _____  _____

**Security Question**          **Answer**

_____             _____

_____             _____

_____             _____

_____             _____

**Business**                    **Contact/Customer Service**

_____        _____

**Web Address**

_____

**Log in/username**    **Password**

_____  _____   _____  _____  _____

_____  _____   _____  _____  _____

_____  _____   _____  _____  _____

_____  _____   _____  _____  _____

**Security Question**          **Answer**

_____             _____

_____             _____

_____             _____

_____             _____

Businesses and Websites

**Business** _____ **Contact/Customer Service** _____

**Web Address** _____

**Log in/username** _____ **Password** _____

_____  _____  _____  _____  _____

_____  _____  _____  _____  _____

_____  _____  _____  _____  _____

_____  _____  _____  _____  _____

**Security Question** _____ **Answer** _____

_____  _____

_____  _____

_____  _____

_____  _____

---

**Business** _____ **Contact/Customer Service** _____

**Web Address** _____

**Log in/username** _____ **Password** _____

_____  _____  _____  _____  _____

_____  _____  _____  _____  _____

_____  _____  _____  _____  _____

_____  _____  _____  _____  _____

**Security Question** _____ **Answer** _____

_____  _____

_____  _____

_____  _____

_____  _____

E

Businesses and Websites

**Businesses and Websites**

Business                    Contact/Customer Service

Web Address

Log in/username      Password

Security Question          Answer

---

Business                    Contact/Customer Service

Web Address

Log in/username      Password

Security Question          Answer

**Business**                              **Contact/Customer Service**

_____        _____

**Web Address**

_____

**Log in/username**      **Password**

_____  _____   _____  _____  _____

_____  _____   _____  _____  _____

_____  _____   _____  _____  _____

_____  _____   _____  _____  _____

**Security Question**                **Answer**

_____        _____

_____        _____

_____        _____

_____        _____

**E**

**Business**                              **Contact/Customer Service**

_____        _____

**Web Address**

_____

**Log in/username**      **Password**

_____  _____   _____  _____  _____

_____  _____   _____  _____  _____

_____  _____   _____  _____  _____

_____  _____   _____  _____  _____

**Security Question**                **Answer**

_____        _____

_____        _____

_____        _____

_____        _____

**Businesses and Websites**

**Business**                    **Contact/Customer Service**

**Web Address**

**Log in/username**        **Password**

**Security Question**              **Answer**

**Business**                    **Contact/Customer Service**

**Web Address**

**Log in/username**        **Password**

**Security Question**              **Answer**

**Business** _____ **Contact/Customer Service** _____

**Web Address** _____

**Log in/username**          **Password**

_____   _____   _____   _____   _____

_____   _____   _____   _____   _____

_____   _____   _____   _____   _____

_____   _____   _____   _____   _____

**Security Question**                    **Answer**

_____            _____

_____            _____

_____            _____

_____            _____

**Business** _____ **Contact/Customer Service** _____

**Web Address** _____

**Log in/username**          **Password**

_____   _____   _____   _____   _____

_____   _____   _____   _____   _____

_____   _____   _____   _____   _____

_____   _____   _____   _____   _____

**Security Question**                    **Answer**

_____            _____

_____            _____

_____            _____

_____            _____

**Businesses and Websites**

Business                    Contact/Customer Service

_____     _____

Web Address

_____

Log in/username      Password

_____    _____    _____    _____    _____

_____    _____    _____    _____    _____

_____    _____    _____    _____    _____

_____    _____    _____    _____    _____

Security Question           Answer

_____     _____

_____     _____

_____     _____

_____     _____

Business                    Contact/Customer Service

_____     _____

Web Address

_____

Log in/username      Password

_____    _____    _____    _____    _____

_____    _____    _____    _____    _____

_____    _____    _____    _____    _____

_____    _____    _____    _____    _____

Security Question           Answer

_____     _____

_____     _____

_____     _____

_____     _____

**Business** _____ **Contact/Customer Service** _____

**Web Address** _____

**Log in/username** _____ **Password** _____

_____ _____ _____ _____ _____

_____ _____ _____ _____ _____

_____ _____ _____ _____ _____

_____ _____ _____ _____ _____

**Security Question** **Answer**

_____ _____

_____ _____

_____ _____

_____ _____

**F**

**Business** _____ **Contact/Customer Service** _____

**Web Address** _____

**Log in/username** _____ **Password** _____

_____ _____ _____ _____ _____

_____ _____ _____ _____ _____

_____ _____ _____ _____ _____

_____ _____ _____ _____ _____

**Security Question** **Answer**

_____ _____

_____ _____

_____ _____

_____ _____

**Businesses and Websites**

**Business**                              **Contact/Customer Service**

_____          _____

**Web Address**

_____

**Log in/username**       **Password**

_____   _____   _____   _____   _____

_____   _____   _____   _____   _____

_____   _____   _____   _____   _____

_____   _____   _____   _____   _____

**Security Question**                      **Answer**

_____          _____

_____          _____

_____          _____

_____          _____

**Business**                              **Contact/Customer Service**

_____          _____

**Web Address**

_____

**Log in/username**       **Password**

_____   _____   _____   _____   _____

_____   _____   _____   _____   _____

_____   _____   _____   _____   _____

_____   _____   _____   _____   _____

**Security Question**                      **Answer**

_____          _____

_____          _____

_____          _____

_____          _____

**Business**        **Contact/Customer Service**

_____    _____

**Web Address**

_____

**Log in/username**    **Password**

_____   _____   _____   _____   _____

_____   _____   _____   _____   _____

_____   _____   _____   _____   _____

_____   _____   _____   _____   _____

**Security Question**      **Answer**

_____    _____

_____    _____

_____    _____

_____    _____

**G**

**Business**        **Contact/Customer Service**

_____    _____

**Web Address**

_____

**Log in/username**    **Password**

_____   _____   _____   _____   _____

_____   _____   _____   _____   _____

_____   _____   _____   _____   _____

_____   _____   _____   _____   _____

**Security Question**      **Answer**

_____    _____

_____    _____

_____    _____

_____    _____

**Businesses and Websites**

**Business** _____      **Contact/Customer Service** _____

**Web Address** _____

**Log in/username**      **Password**

_____ _____ _____ _____ _____
_____ _____ _____ _____ _____
_____ _____ _____ _____ _____
_____ _____ _____ _____ _____

**Security Question**      **Answer**

**G**

---

**Business** _____      **Contact/Customer Service** _____

**Web Address** _____

**Log in/username**      **Password**

_____ _____ _____ _____ _____
_____ _____ _____ _____ _____
_____ _____ _____ _____ _____
_____ _____ _____ _____ _____

**Security Question**      **Answer**

**Businesses and Websites**

**Business** _____   **Contact/Customer Service** _____

**Web Address** _____

**Log in/username**     **Password**

_____  _____  _____  _____  _____

_____  _____  _____  _____  _____

_____  _____  _____  _____  _____

_____  _____  _____  _____  _____

**Security Question**     **Answer**

_____     _____

_____     _____

_____     _____

_____     _____

---

**Business** _____   **Contact/Customer Service** _____

**Web Address** _____

**Log in/username**     **Password**

_____  _____  _____  _____  _____

_____  _____  _____  _____  _____

_____  _____  _____  _____  _____

_____  _____  _____  _____  _____

**Security Question**     **Answer**

_____     _____

_____     _____

_____     _____

_____     _____

G

Businesses and Websites

**Business** **Contact/Customer Service**

_____ _____

**Web Address**

_____

**Log in/username** **Password**

_____ _____ _____ _____ _____

_____ _____ _____ _____ _____

_____ _____ _____ _____ _____

_____ _____ _____ _____ _____

**Security Question** **Answer**

_____ _____

_____ _____

_____ _____

_____ _____

**Business** **Contact/Customer Service**

_____ _____

**Web Address**

_____

**Log in/username** **Password**

_____ _____ _____ _____ _____

_____ _____ _____ _____ _____

_____ _____ _____ _____ _____

_____ _____ _____ _____ _____

**Security Question** **Answer**

_____ _____

_____ _____

_____ _____

_____ _____

**Business** _____  **Contact/Customer Service**
_____

**Web Address**
_____

**Log in/username**     **Password**
_____  _____  _____  _____  _____
_____  _____  _____  _____  _____
_____  _____  _____  _____  _____
_____  _____  _____  _____  _____

**Security Question**        **Answer**
_____                   _____
_____                   _____
_____                   _____
_____                   _____

**Business** _____  **Contact/Customer Service**
_____

**Web Address**
_____

**Log in/username**     **Password**
_____  _____  _____  _____  _____
_____  _____  _____  _____  _____
_____  _____  _____  _____  _____
_____  _____  _____  _____  _____

**Security Question**        **Answer**
_____                   _____
_____                   _____
_____                   _____
_____                   _____

H

Businesses and Websites

**Business**  **Contact/Customer Service**

_____  _____

**Web Address**

_____

**Log in/username**  **Password**

_____  _____  _____  _____  _____
_____  _____  _____  _____  _____
_____  _____  _____  _____  _____
_____  _____  _____  _____  _____

**Security Question**  **Answer**

_____  _____
_____  _____
_____  _____
_____  _____

**Business**  **Contact/Customer Service**

_____  _____

**Web Address**

_____

**Log in/username**  **Password**

_____  _____  _____  _____  _____
_____  _____  _____  _____  _____
_____  _____  _____  _____  _____
_____  _____  _____  _____  _____

**Security Question**  **Answer**

_____  _____
_____  _____
_____  _____
_____  _____

**Businesses and Websites**

**Business** _____ **Contact/Customer Service** _____

**Web Address** _____

**Log in/username** _____ **Password** _____

_____ _____ _____ _____ _____
_____ _____ _____ _____ _____
_____ _____ _____ _____ _____
_____ _____ _____ _____ _____

**Security Question** _____ **Answer** _____

_____ _____
_____ _____
_____ _____
_____ _____

---

**Business** _____ **Contact/Customer Service** _____

**Web Address** _____

**Log in/username** _____ **Password** _____

_____ _____ _____ _____ _____
_____ _____ _____ _____ _____
_____ _____ _____ _____ _____
_____ _____ _____ _____ _____

**Security Question** _____ **Answer** _____

_____ _____
_____ _____
_____ _____
_____ _____

H

**Businesses and Websites**

**Business** _____ **Contact/Customer Service** _____

**Web Address** _____

**Log in/username**　　　**Password**

_____ ___ ___ ___ ___

_____ ___ ___ ___ ___

_____ ___ ___ ___ ___

_____ ___ ___ ___ ___

**Security Question**　　　　　　**Answer**

_____　　　_____

_____　　　_____

_____　　　_____

_____　　　_____

**Business** _____ **Contact/Customer Service** _____

**Web Address** _____

**Log in/username**　　　**Password**

_____ ___ ___ ___ ___

_____ ___ ___ ___ ___

_____ ___ ___ ___ ___

_____ ___ ___ ___ ___

**Security Question**　　　　　　**Answer**

_____　　　_____

_____　　　_____

_____　　　_____

_____　　　_____

**Businesses and Websites**

**Business** _____ **Contact/Customer Service** _____

**Web Address** _____

**Log in/username** _____ **Password** _____

_____  _____  _____  _____  _____

_____  _____  _____  _____  _____

_____  _____  _____  _____  _____

_____  _____  _____  _____  _____

**Security Question** _____  **Answer** _____

_____  _____

_____  _____

_____  _____

_____  _____

**Business** _____ **Contact/Customer Service** _____

**Web Address** _____

**Log in/username** _____ **Password** _____

_____  _____  _____  _____  _____

_____  _____  _____  _____  _____

_____  _____  _____  _____  _____

_____  _____  _____  _____  _____

**Security Question** _____  **Answer** _____

_____  _____

_____  _____

_____  _____

_____  _____

**Businesses and Websites**

**Business** _____  **Contact/Customer Service** _____

**Web Address** _____

**Log in/username**          **Password**

_____    _____    _____    _____    _____

_____    _____    _____    _____    _____

_____    _____    _____    _____    _____

_____    _____    _____    _____    _____

**Security Question**                    **Answer**

_____                   _____

_____                   _____

_____                   _____

_____                   _____

**Business** _____  **Contact/Customer Service** _____

**Web Address** _____

**Log in/username**          **Password**

_____    _____    _____    _____    _____

_____    _____    _____    _____    _____

_____    _____    _____    _____    _____

_____    _____    _____    _____    _____

**Security Question**                    **Answer**

_____                   _____

_____                   _____

_____                   _____

_____                   _____

**Businesses and Websites**

**Business** _____ **Contact/Customer Service** _____

**Web Address** _____

**Log in/username** _____ **Password** _____

_____ _____ _____ _____ _____

_____ _____ _____ _____ _____

_____ _____ _____ _____ _____

_____ _____ _____ _____ _____

**Security Question** _____ **Answer** _____

_____ _____

_____ _____

_____ _____

**Business** _____ **Contact/Customer Service** _____

**Web Address** _____

**Log in/username** _____ **Password** _____

_____ _____ _____ _____ _____

_____ _____ _____ _____ _____

_____ _____ _____ _____ _____

_____ _____ _____ _____ _____

**Security Question** _____ **Answer** _____

_____ _____

_____ _____

_____ _____

**Businesses and Websites**

**Business**                    **Contact/Customer Service**

_____    _____

**Web Address**

_____

**Log in/username**        **Password**

_____  _____  _____  _____  _____

_____  _____  _____  _____  _____

_____  _____  _____  _____  _____

_____  _____  _____  _____  _____

**Security Question**            **Answer**

_____    _____

_____    _____

_____    _____

_____    _____

**Business**                    **Contact/Customer Service**

_____    _____

**Web Address**

_____

**Log in/username**        **Password**

_____  _____  _____  _____  _____

_____  _____  _____  _____  _____

_____  _____  _____  _____  _____

_____  _____  _____  _____  _____

**Security Question**            **Answer**

_____    _____

_____    _____

_____    _____

_____    _____

**J**

**Businesses and Websites**

**Business**             **Contact/Customer Service**

_____

**Web Address**

_____

**Log in/username**     **Password**

_____  _____  _____  _____  _____

_____  _____  _____  _____  _____

_____  _____  _____  _____  _____

_____  _____  _____  _____  _____

**Security Question**       **Answer**

_____  _____

_____  _____

_____  _____

_____  _____

**J**

---

**Business**             **Contact/Customer Service**

_____

**Web Address**

_____

**Log in/username**     **Password**

_____  _____  _____  _____  _____

_____  _____  _____  _____  _____

_____  _____  _____  _____  _____

_____  _____  _____  _____  _____

**Security Question**       **Answer**

_____  _____

_____  _____

_____  _____

_____  _____

**Businesses and Websites**

**Business** _____ **Contact/Customer Service** _____

**Web Address** _____

**Log in/username** _____ **Password** _____

_____ _____ _____ _____ _____

_____ _____ _____ _____ _____

_____ _____ _____ _____ _____

_____ _____ _____ _____ _____

**J**

**Security Question** _____ **Answer** _____

_____ _____

_____ _____

_____ _____

_____ _____

---

**Business** _____ **Contact/Customer Service** _____

**Web Address** _____

**Log in/username** _____ **Password** _____

_____ _____ _____ _____ _____

_____ _____ _____ _____ _____

_____ _____ _____ _____ _____

_____ _____ _____ _____ _____

**Businesses and Websites**

**Security Question** _____ **Answer** _____

_____ _____

_____ _____

_____ _____

_____ _____

**Business** _____ **Contact/Customer Service**
_____          _____

**Web Address**
_____

**Log in/username**      **Password**
_____  _____  _____  _____  _____
_____  _____  _____  _____  _____
_____  _____  _____  _____  _____
_____  _____  _____  _____  _____

**Security Question**          **Answer**
_____    _____
_____    _____
_____    _____
_____    _____

**J**

**Business** _____ **Contact/Customer Service**
_____          _____

**Web Address**
_____

**Log in/username**      **Password**
_____  _____  _____  _____  _____
_____  _____  _____  _____  _____
_____  _____  _____  _____  _____
_____  _____  _____  _____  _____

**Security Question**          **Answer**
_____    _____
_____    _____
_____    _____
_____    _____

**Businesses and Websites**

**Business**                          **Contact/Customer Service**

_____          _____

**Web Address**

_____

**Log in/username**     **Password**

_____  _____  _____  _____  _____

_____  _____  _____  _____  _____

_____  _____  _____  _____  _____

_____  _____  _____  _____  _____

**Security Question**              **Answer**

_____          _____

_____          _____

_____          _____

_____          _____

**Business**                          **Contact/Customer Service**

_____          _____

**Web Address**

_____

**Log in/username**     **Password**

_____  _____  _____  _____  _____

_____  _____  _____  _____  _____

_____  _____  _____  _____  _____

_____  _____  _____  _____  _____

**Security Question**              **Answer**

_____          _____

_____          _____

_____          _____

_____          _____

**Businesses and Websites**

**Business** _____    **Contact/Customer Service**

_____    _____

**Web Address**

_____

**Log in/username**    **Password**

_____    _____  _____  _____  _____

_____    _____  _____  _____  _____

_____    _____  _____  _____  _____

_____    _____  _____  _____  _____

**Security Question**    **Answer**

_____    _____

_____    _____

_____    _____

_____    _____

**Business** _____    **Contact/Customer Service**

_____    _____

**Web Address**

_____

**Log in/username**    **Password**

_____    _____  _____  _____  _____

_____    _____  _____  _____  _____

_____    _____  _____  _____  _____

_____    _____  _____  _____  _____

**Security Question**    **Answer**

_____    _____

_____    _____

_____    _____

_____    _____

K

Businesses and Websites

**Business**                    **Contact/Customer Service**

_____    _____

**Web Address**

_____

**Log in/username**    **Password**

_____  _____  _____  _____  _____

_____  _____  _____  _____  _____

_____  _____  _____  _____  _____

_____  _____  _____  _____  _____

**Security Question**              **Answer**

_____    _____

_____    _____

_____    _____

_____    _____

**Business**                    **Contact/Customer Service**

_____    _____

**Web Address**

_____

**Log in/username**    **Password**

_____  _____  _____  _____  _____

_____  _____  _____  _____  _____

_____  _____  _____  _____  _____

_____  _____  _____  _____  _____

**Security Question**              **Answer**

_____    _____

_____    _____

_____    _____

_____    _____

**Business**             **Contact/Customer Service**

_____     _____

**Web Address**

_____

**Log in/username**     **Password**

_____   _____   _____   _____   _____

_____   _____   _____   _____   _____

_____   _____   _____   _____   _____

_____   _____   _____   _____   _____

**Security Question**        **Answer**

_____     _____

_____     _____

_____     _____

_____     _____

**K**

**Business**             **Contact/Customer Service**

_____     _____

**Web Address**

_____

**Log in/username**     **Password**

_____   _____   _____   _____   _____

_____   _____   _____   _____   _____

_____   _____   _____   _____   _____

_____   _____   _____   _____   _____

**Security Question**        **Answer**

_____     _____

_____     _____

_____     _____

_____     _____

**Businesses and Websites**

**Business**  **Contact/Customer Service**

_____  _____

**Web Address**

_____

**Log in/username**  **Password**

_____  _____  _____  _____  _____

_____  _____  _____  _____  _____

_____  _____  _____  _____  _____

_____  _____  _____  _____  _____

**Security Question**  **Answer**

_____  _____

_____  _____

_____  _____

_____  _____

**Business**  **Contact/Customer Service**

_____  _____

**Web Address**

_____

**Log in/username**  **Password**

_____  _____  _____  _____  _____

_____  _____  _____  _____  _____

_____  _____  _____  _____  _____

_____  _____  _____  _____  _____

**Security Question**  **Answer**

_____  _____

_____  _____

_____  _____

_____  _____

**Business** _____  **Contact/Customer Service**
_____                _____

**Web Address**
_____

**Log in/username**     **Password**
_____    _____    _____    _____    _____
_____    _____    _____    _____    _____
_____    _____    _____    _____    _____
_____    _____    _____    _____    _____

**Security Question**              **Answer**
_____            _____
_____            _____
_____            _____
_____            _____

**Business** _____  **Contact/Customer Service**
_____                _____

**Web Address**
_____

**Log in/username**     **Password**
_____    _____    _____    _____    _____
_____    _____    _____    _____    _____
_____    _____    _____    _____    _____
_____    _____    _____    _____    _____

**Security Question**              **Answer**
_____            _____
_____            _____
_____            _____
_____            _____

**Businesses and Websites**

**Business**                      **Contact/Customer Service**

_____    _____

**Web Address**

_____

**Log in/username**     **Password**

_____ _____ _____ _____ _____

_____ _____ _____ _____ _____

_____ _____ _____ _____ _____

_____ _____ _____ _____ _____

**Security Question**         **Answer**

_____      _____

_____      _____

_____      _____

_____      _____

**L**

---

**Business**                      **Contact/Customer Service**

_____    _____

**Web Address**

_____

**Log in/username**     **Password**

_____ _____ _____ _____ _____

_____ _____ _____ _____ _____

_____ _____ _____ _____ _____

_____ _____ _____ _____ _____

**Security Question**         **Answer**

_____      _____

_____      _____

_____      _____

_____      _____

**Businesses and Websites**

**Business** _____ **Contact/Customer Service** _____

**Web Address** _____

**Log in/username** _____ **Password** _____

_____ _____ _____ _____ _____

_____ _____ _____ _____ _____

_____ _____ _____ _____ _____

_____ _____ _____ _____ _____

**Security Question** _____ **Answer** _____

_____ _____

_____ _____

_____ _____

_____ _____

**L**

**Business** _____ **Contact/Customer Service** _____

**Web Address** _____

**Log in/username** _____ **Password** _____

_____ _____ _____ _____ _____

_____ _____ _____ _____ _____

_____ _____ _____ _____ _____

_____ _____ _____ _____ _____

**Security Question** _____ **Answer** _____

_____ _____

_____ _____

_____ _____

_____ _____

**Businesses and Websites**

**Business**                                    **Contact/Customer Service**

_____        _____

**Web Address**

_____

**Log in/username**         **Password**

_____    _____    _____   _____   _____

_____    _____    _____   _____   _____

_____    _____    _____   _____   _____

_____    _____    _____   _____   _____

**Security Question**                    **Answer**

_____        _____

_____        _____

_____        _____

_____        _____

**Business**                                    **Contact/Customer Service**

_____        _____

**Web Address**

_____

**Log in/username**         **Password**

_____    _____    _____   _____   _____

_____    _____    _____   _____   _____

_____    _____    _____   _____   _____

_____    _____    _____   _____   _____

**Security Question**                    **Answer**

_____        _____

_____        _____

_____        _____

_____        _____

**Businesses and Websites**

**Business**               **Contact/Customer Service**

_____    _____

**Web Address**

_____

**Log in/username**      **Password**

_____   _____   _____   _____   _____

_____   _____   _____   _____   _____

_____   _____   _____   _____   _____

_____   _____   _____   _____   _____

**Security Question**         **Answer**

_____    _____

_____    _____

_____    _____

_____    _____

## M

**Business**               **Contact/Customer Service**

_____    _____

**Web Address**

_____

**Log in/username**      **Password**

_____   _____   _____   _____   _____

_____   _____   _____   _____   _____

_____   _____   _____   _____   _____

_____   _____   _____   _____   _____

**Security Question**         **Answer**

_____    _____

_____    _____

_____    _____

_____    _____

**Businesses and Websites**

**Business**                    **Contact/Customer Service**

_____         _____

**Web Address**

_____

**Log in/username**      **Password**

_____  _____  _____  _____  _____

_____  _____  _____  _____  _____

_____  _____  _____  _____  _____

_____  _____  _____  _____  _____

**Security Question**              **Answer**

_____         _____

_____         _____

_____         _____

_____         _____

**Business**                    **Contact/Customer Service**

_____         _____

**Web Address**

_____

**Log in/username**      **Password**

_____  _____  _____  _____  _____

_____  _____  _____  _____  _____

_____  _____  _____  _____  _____

_____  _____  _____  _____  _____

**Security Question**              **Answer**

_____         _____

_____         _____

_____         _____

_____         _____

**Business** _____ **Contact/Customer Service**

_____ _____

**Web Address**

_____

**Log in/username**     **Password**

_____ _____ _____ _____ _____

_____ _____ _____ _____ _____

_____ _____ _____ _____ _____

_____ _____ _____ _____ _____

**Security Question**                **Answer**

_____      _____

_____      _____

_____      _____

_____      _____

**Business** _____ **Contact/Customer Service**

_____ _____

**Web Address**

_____

**Log in/username**     **Password**

_____ _____ _____ _____ _____

_____ _____ _____ _____ _____

_____ _____ _____ _____ _____

_____ _____ _____ _____ _____

**Security Question**                **Answer**

_____      _____

_____      _____

_____      _____

_____      _____

**Businesses and Websites**

**N**

---

Business                          Contact/Customer Service

Web Address

Log in/username          Password

Security Question                 Answer

---

Business                          Contact/Customer Service

Web Address

Log in/username          Password

Security Question                 Answer

---

**Business**                **Contact/Customer Service**

_____    _____

**Web Address**

_____

**Log in/username**      **Password**

_____ _____ _____ _____ _____

_____ _____ _____ _____ _____

_____ _____ _____ _____ _____

_____ _____ _____ _____ _____

**Security Question**        **Answer**

_____    _____

_____    _____

_____    _____

_____    _____

**N**

**Business**                **Contact/Customer Service**

_____    _____

**Web Address**

_____

**Log in/username**      **Password**

_____ _____ _____ _____ _____

_____ _____ _____ _____ _____

_____ _____ _____ _____ _____

_____ _____ _____ _____ _____

**Security Question**        **Answer**

_____    _____

_____    _____

_____    _____

_____    _____

**N**

**Business**                    **Contact/Customer Service**

_____        _____

**Web Address**

_____

**Log in/username**      **Password**

_____    _____    _____   _____   _____

_____    _____    _____   _____   _____

_____    _____    _____   _____   _____

_____    _____    _____   _____   _____

**Security Question**              **Answer**

_____        _____

_____        _____

_____        _____

_____        _____

**Business**                    **Contact/Customer Service**

_____        _____

**Web Address**

_____

**Log in/username**      **Password**

_____    _____    _____   _____   _____

_____    _____    _____   _____   _____

_____    _____    _____   _____   _____

_____    _____    _____   _____   _____

**Security Question**              **Answer**

_____        _____

_____        _____

_____        _____

_____        _____

**Business**                    **Contact/Customer Service**

_____    _____

**Web Address**

_____

**Log in/username**    **Password**

_____  _____  _____  _____  _____

_____  _____  _____  _____  _____

_____  _____  _____  _____  _____

_____  _____  _____  _____  _____

**Security Question**                    **Answer**

_____    _____

_____    _____

_____    _____

_____    _____

**Business**                    **Contact/Customer Service**

_____    _____

**Web Address**

_____

**Log in/username**    **Password**

_____  _____  _____  _____  _____

_____  _____  _____  _____  _____

_____  _____  _____  _____  _____

_____  _____  _____  _____  _____

**Security Question**                    **Answer**

_____    _____

_____    _____

_____    _____

_____    _____

**Business**            **Contact/Customer Service**

_____    _____

**Web Address**

_____

**Log in/username**     **Password**

_____   _____   _____   _____   _____

_____   _____   _____   _____   _____

_____   _____   _____   _____   _____

_____   _____   _____   _____   _____

**Security Question**           **Answer**

_____    _____

_____    _____

_____    _____

_____    _____

**O**

**Business**            **Contact/Customer Service**

_____    _____

**Web Address**

_____

**Log in/username**     **Password**

_____   _____   _____   _____   _____

_____   _____   _____   _____   _____

_____   _____   _____   _____   _____

_____   _____   _____   _____   _____

**Security Question**           **Answer**

_____    _____

_____    _____

_____    _____

_____    _____

**Business**  **Contact/Customer Service**

_____  _____

**Web Address**

_____

**Log in/username**  **Password**

_____  ____  ____  ____  ____

_____  ____  ____  ____  ____

_____  ____  ____  ____  ____

_____  ____  ____  ____  ____

**Security Question**  **Answer**

_____  _____

_____  _____

_____  _____

_____  _____

**Business**  **Contact/Customer Service**  O

_____  _____

**Web Address**

_____

**Log in/username**  **Password**

_____  ____  ____  ____  ____

_____  ____  ____  ____  ____

_____  ____  ____  ____  ____

_____  ____  ____  ____  ____

**Security Question**  **Answer**

_____  _____

_____  _____

_____  _____

_____  _____

**Businesses and Websites**

---

**Business**                                    **Contact/Customer Service**

_____          _____

**Web Address**

_____

**Log in/username**        **Password**

_____    _____    _____    _____    _____

_____    _____    _____    _____    _____

_____    _____    _____    _____    _____

_____    _____    _____    _____    _____

**Security Question**                     **Answer**

_____          _____

_____          _____

_____          _____

_____          _____

---

O

**Business**                                    **Contact/Customer Service**

_____          _____

**Web Address**

_____

**Log in/username**        **Password**

_____    _____    _____    _____    _____

_____    _____    _____    _____    _____

_____    _____    _____    _____    _____

_____    _____    _____    _____    _____

**Security Question**                     **Answer**

_____          _____

_____          _____

_____          _____

_____          _____

---

**Business** _____ **Contact/Customer Service** _____

**Web Address** _____

**Log in/username** _____ **Password** _____

_____

_____

_____

**Security Question** _____ **Answer** _____

**Business** _____ **Contact/Customer Service** _____

O

**Web Address** _____

**Log in/username** _____ **Password** _____

_____

_____

_____

**Security Question** _____ **Answer** _____

**Business**                    **Contact/Customer Service**

_____    _____

**Web Address**

_____

**Log in/username**        **Password**

_____  _____    _____  _____  _____

_____  _____    _____  _____  _____

_____  _____    _____  _____  _____

_____  _____    _____  _____  _____

**Security Question**              **Answer**

_____    _____

_____    _____

_____    _____

_____    _____

**P**

**Business**                    **Contact/Customer Service**

_____    _____

**Web Address**

_____

**Log in/username**        **Password**

_____  _____    _____  _____  _____

_____  _____    _____  _____  _____

_____  _____    _____  _____  _____

_____  _____    _____  _____  _____

**Security Question**              **Answer**

_____    _____

_____    _____

_____    _____

_____    _____

**Business**                    **Contact/Customer Service**

_____        _____

**Web Address**

_____

**Log in/username**      **Password**

_____  _____   _____  _____  _____
_____  _____   _____  _____  _____
_____  _____   _____  _____  _____
_____  _____   _____  _____  _____

**Security Question**              **Answer**

_____        _____
_____        _____
_____        _____
_____        _____

**Business**                    **Contact/Customer Service**

_____        _____

**Web Address**

_____

**Log in/username**      **Password**

_____  _____   _____  _____  _____
_____  _____   _____  _____  _____
_____  _____   _____  _____  _____
_____  _____   _____  _____  _____

**Security Question**              **Answer**

_____        _____
_____        _____
_____        _____
_____        _____

**P**

**Business**                    **Contact/Customer Service**

_____         _____

**Web Address**

_____

**Log in/username**     **Password**

_____  _____  _____  _____  _____
_____  _____  _____  _____  _____
_____  _____  _____  _____  _____
_____  _____  _____  _____  _____

**Security Question**              **Answer**

_____         _____
_____         _____
_____         _____
_____         _____

**P**

**Business**                    **Contact/Customer Service**

_____         _____

**Web Address**

_____

**Log in/username**     **Password**

_____  _____  _____  _____  _____
_____  _____  _____  _____  _____
_____  _____  _____  _____  _____
_____  _____  _____  _____  _____

**Security Question**              **Answer**

_____         _____
_____         _____
_____         _____
_____         _____

**Business**                    **Contact/Customer Service**
_____    _____

**Web Address**
_____

**Log in/username**     **Password**
_____  _____   _____  _____  _____
_____  _____   _____  _____  _____
_____  _____   _____  _____  _____
_____  _____   _____  _____  _____

**Security Question**              **Answer**
_____    _____
_____    _____
_____    _____
_____    _____

**Business**                    **Contact/Customer Service**
_____    _____

**Web Address**
_____

**Log in/username**     **Password**
_____  _____   _____  _____  _____
_____  _____   _____  _____  _____
_____  _____   _____  _____  _____
_____  _____   _____  _____  _____

**Security Question**              **Answer**
_____    _____
_____    _____
_____    _____
_____    _____

**P**

**Business**　　　　　　　　　**Contact/Customer Service**

_____　　_____

**Web Address**

_____

**Log in/username**　　**Password**

_____　____　____　____　____

_____　____　____　____　____

_____　____　____　____　____

_____　____　____　____　____

**Security Question**　　　　　**Answer**

_____　　_____

_____　　_____

_____　　_____

_____　　_____

**Q**

**Business**　　　　　　　　　**Contact/Customer Service**

_____　　_____

**Web Address**

_____

**Log in/username**　　**Password**

_____　____　____　____　____

_____　____　____　____　____

_____　____　____　____　____

_____　____　____　____　____

**Security Question**　　　　　**Answer**

_____　　_____

_____　　_____

_____　　_____

_____　　_____

**Business**                    **Contact/Customer Service**

_____    _____

**Web Address**

_____

**Log in/username**    **Password**

_____  _____  _____  _____  _____

_____  _____  _____  _____  _____

_____  _____  _____  _____  _____

_____  _____  _____  _____  _____

**Security Question**          **Answer**

_____    _____

_____    _____

_____    _____

_____    _____

**Business**                    **Contact/Customer Service**

_____    _____

**Web Address**

_____

**Log in/username**    **Password**

_____  _____  _____  _____  _____

_____  _____  _____  _____  _____

_____  _____  _____  _____  _____

_____  _____  _____  _____  _____

**Security Question**          **Answer**

_____    _____

_____    _____

_____    _____

_____    _____

**Q**

**Business**                    **Contact/Customer Service**

_____    _____

**Web Address**

_____

**Log in/username**     **Password**

_____   _____   _____   _____   _____
_____   _____   _____   _____   _____
_____   _____   _____   _____   _____
_____   _____   _____   _____   _____

**Security Question**              **Answer**

_____    _____
_____    _____
_____    _____
_____    _____

**Q**

**Business**                    **Contact/Customer Service**

_____    _____

**Web Address**

_____

**Log in/username**     **Password**

_____   _____   _____   _____   _____
_____   _____   _____   _____   _____
_____   _____   _____   _____   _____
_____   _____   _____   _____   _____

**Security Question**              **Answer**

_____    _____
_____    _____
_____    _____
_____    _____

**Business**                 **Contact/Customer Service**

_____    _____

**Web Address**

_____

**Log in/username**      **Password**

_____   _____   _____   _____   _____

_____   _____   _____   _____   _____

_____   _____   _____   _____   _____

_____   _____   _____   _____   _____

**Security Question**            **Answer**

_____    _____

_____    _____

_____    _____

_____    _____

---

**Business**                 **Contact/Customer Service**

_____    _____

**Web Address**

_____

**Log in/username**      **Password**

**Q**

_____   _____   _____   _____   _____

_____   _____   _____   _____   _____

_____   _____   _____   _____   _____

_____   _____   _____   _____   _____

**Security Question**            **Answer**

_____    _____

_____    _____

_____    _____

_____    _____

**Business**                    **Contact/Customer Service**

_____        _____

**Web Address**

_____

**Log in/username**      **Password**

_____  _____  _____  _____  _____
_____  _____  _____  _____  _____
_____  _____  _____  _____  _____
_____  _____  _____  _____  _____

**Security Question**            **Answer**

_____        _____
_____        _____
_____        _____
_____        _____

**R**

**Business**                    **Contact/Customer Service**

_____        _____

**Web Address**

_____

**Log in/username**      **Password**

_____  _____  _____  _____  _____
_____  _____  _____  _____  _____
_____  _____  _____  _____  _____
_____  _____  _____  _____  _____

**Security Question**            **Answer**

_____        _____
_____        _____
_____        _____
_____        _____

**Business**                  **Contact/Customer Service**

_____    _____

**Web Address**

_____

**Log in/username**      **Password**

_____ _____ _____ _____ _____

_____ _____ _____ _____ _____

_____ _____ _____ _____ _____

_____ _____ _____ _____ _____

**Security Question**           **Answer**

_____    _____

_____    _____

_____    _____

_____    _____

---

**Business**                  **Contact/Customer Service**

_____    _____

**Web Address**

_____

**Log in/username**      **Password**               **R**

_____ _____ _____ _____ _____

_____ _____ _____ _____ _____

_____ _____ _____ _____ _____

_____ _____ _____ _____ _____

**Security Question**           **Answer**

_____    _____

_____    _____

_____    _____

_____    _____

**Business**                                    **Contact/Customer Service**
_____        _____

**Web Address**
_____

**Log in/username**        **Password**
_____  _____  _____  _____  _____
_____  _____  _____  _____  _____
_____  _____  _____  _____  _____
_____  _____  _____  _____  _____

**Security Question**                    **Answer**
_____        _____
_____        _____
_____        _____
_____        _____

**Business**                                    **Contact/Customer Service**
_____        _____

**Web Address**
_____

**R**     **Log in/username**        **Password**
_____  _____  _____  _____  _____
_____  _____  _____  _____  _____
_____  _____  _____  _____  _____
_____  _____  _____  _____  _____

**Security Question**                    **Answer**
_____        _____
_____        _____
_____        _____
_____        _____

**Business**                          **Contact/Customer Service**

_____              _____

**Web Address**

_____

**Log in/username**        **Password**

_____  _____  _____  _____  _____

_____  _____  _____  _____  _____

_____  _____  _____  _____  _____

_____  _____  _____  _____  _____

**Security Question**                  **Answer**

_____              _____

_____              _____

_____              _____

_____              _____

**Business**                          **Contact/Customer Service**

_____              _____

**Web Address**

_____

**Log in/username**        **Password**                          R

_____  _____  _____  _____  _____

_____  _____  _____  _____  _____

_____  _____  _____  _____  _____

_____  _____  _____  _____  _____

**Security Question**                  **Answer**

_____              _____

_____              _____

_____              _____

_____              _____

**Business**

**Contact/Customer Service**

_____

**Web Address**

_____

**Log in/username**          **Password**

_____  _____  _____  _____  _____

_____  _____  _____  _____  _____

_____  _____  _____  _____  _____

_____  _____  _____  _____  _____

**Security Question**

**Answer**

_____          _____

_____          _____

_____          _____

_____          _____

---

**S**

**Business**

**Contact/Customer Service**

_____

**Web Address**

_____

**Log in/username**          **Password**

_____  _____  _____  _____  _____

_____  _____  _____  _____  _____

_____  _____  _____  _____  _____

_____  _____  _____  _____  _____

**Security Question**

**Answer**

_____          _____

_____          _____

_____          _____

_____          _____

**Business**                    **Contact/Customer Service**

_____         _____

**Web Address**

_____

**Log in/username**      **Password**

_____  _____    _____  _____  _____

_____  _____    _____  _____  _____

_____  _____    _____  _____  _____

_____  _____    _____  _____  _____

**Security Question**            **Answer**

_____         _____

_____         _____

_____         _____

_____         _____


**Business**                    **Contact/Customer Service**

_____         _____

**Web Address**

_____

**Log in/username**      **Password**

_____  _____    _____  _____  _____

_____  _____    _____  _____  _____

_____  _____    _____  _____  _____

_____  _____    _____  _____  _____

**Security Question**            **Answer**

_____         _____

_____         _____

_____         _____

_____         _____

**S**

**Business** _____  **Contact/Customer Service** _____

**Web Address** _____

**Log in/username**          **Password**

_____  _____  _____  ____  _____

_____  _____  _____  ____  _____

_____  _____  _____  ____  _____

_____  _____  _____  ____  _____

**Security Question**          **Answer**

_____          _____

_____          _____

_____          _____

_____          _____

**Business** _____  **Contact/Customer Service** _____

**Web Address** _____

**S**

**Log in/username**          **Password**

_____  _____  _____  ____  _____

_____  _____  _____  ____  _____

_____  _____  _____  ____  _____

_____  _____  _____  ____  _____

**Security Question**          **Answer**

_____          _____

_____          _____

_____          _____

_____          _____

**Business** _____ **Contact/Customer Service** _____

**Web Address** _____

**Log in/username**      **Password**

_____ _____ _____ _____ _____

_____ _____ _____ _____ _____

_____ _____ _____ _____ _____

_____ _____ _____ _____ _____

**Security Question**      **Answer**

_____     _____

_____     _____

_____     _____

_____     _____

**Business** _____ **Contact/Customer Service** _____

**Web Address** _____

**Log in/username**      **Password**

_____ _____ _____ _____ _____

_____ _____ _____ _____ _____

_____ _____ _____ _____ _____

_____ _____ _____ _____ _____

**S**

**Security Question**      **Answer**

_____     _____

_____     _____

_____     _____

_____     _____

**Business**                    **Contact/Customer Service**
_____        _____

**Web Address**
_____

**Log in/username**      **Password**
_____    _____    _____  _____  _____
_____    _____    _____  _____  _____
_____    _____    _____  _____  _____
_____    _____    _____  _____  _____

**Security Question**            **Answer**
_____        _____
_____        _____
_____        _____
_____        _____

**Business**                    **Contact/Customer Service**
_____        _____

**Web Address**
_____

**Log in/username**      **Password**
_____    _____    _____  _____  _____
_____    _____    _____  _____  _____
_____    _____    _____  _____  _____
_____    _____    _____  _____  _____

**Security Question**            **Answer**
_____        _____
_____        _____
_____        _____
_____        _____

T

**Business**                    **Contact/Customer Service**

_____        _____

**Web Address**

_____

**Log in/username**      **Password**

_____    _____    _____    _____    _____

_____    _____    _____    _____    _____

_____    _____    _____    _____    _____

_____    _____    _____    _____    _____

**Security Question**        **Answer**

_____    _____

_____    _____

_____    _____

_____    _____

**Business**                    **Contact/Customer Service**

_____        _____

**Web Address**

_____

**Log in/username**      **Password**

_____    _____    _____    _____    _____

_____    _____    _____    _____    _____

_____    _____    _____    _____    _____

_____    _____    _____    _____    _____

**Security Question**        **Answer**

_____    _____

_____    _____

_____    _____

_____    _____

**T**

79

**Business**                          **Contact/Customer Service**

_____          _____

**Web Address**

_____

**Log in/username**      **Password**

_____  _____  _____  _____  _____
_____  _____  _____  _____  _____
_____  _____  _____  _____  _____
_____  _____  _____  _____  _____

**Security Question**              **Answer**

_____          _____
_____          _____
_____          _____
_____          _____

**Business**                          **Contact/Customer Service**

_____          _____

**Web Address**

_____

**Log in/username**      **Password**

_____  _____  _____  _____  _____
_____  _____  _____  _____  _____
_____  _____  _____  _____  _____
_____  _____  _____  _____  _____

**Security Question**              **Answer**

_____          _____
_____          _____
_____          _____
_____          _____

T

**Business**                          **Contact/Customer Service**

_____              _____

**Web Address**

_____

**Log in/username**     **Password**

_____  _____  _____  _____  _____

_____  _____  _____  _____  _____

_____  _____  _____  _____  _____

_____  _____  _____  _____  _____

**Security Question**                 **Answer**

_____              _____

_____              _____

_____              _____

_____              _____

---

**Business**                          **Contact/Customer Service**

_____              _____

**Web Address**

_____

**Log in/username**     **Password**

_____  _____  _____  _____  _____

_____  _____  _____  _____  _____

_____  _____  _____  _____  _____

_____  _____  _____  _____  _____

**Security Question**                 **Answer**

_____              _____

_____              _____

_____              _____

_____              _____

T

**Business**                    **Contact/Customer Service**

_____          _____

**Web Address**

_____

**Log in/username**     **Password**

_____    _____   _____  _____  _____
_____    _____   _____  _____  _____
_____    _____   _____  _____  _____
_____    _____   _____  _____  _____

**Security Question**              **Answer**

_____            _____
_____            _____
_____            _____
_____            _____

**Business**                    **Contact/Customer Service**

_____          _____

**Web Address**

_____

**Log in/username**     **Password**

_____    _____   _____  _____  _____
_____    _____   _____  _____  _____
_____    _____   _____  _____  _____
_____    _____   _____  _____  _____

**Security Question**              **Answer**

_____            _____
_____            _____
_____            _____
_____            _____

U

**Business**                    **Contact/Customer Service**
_____        _____

**Web Address**
_____

**Log in/username**      **Password**
_____  _____   _____  _____  _____
_____  _____   _____  _____  _____
_____  _____   _____  _____  _____
_____  _____   _____  _____  _____

**Security Question**            **Answer**
_____        _____
_____        _____
_____        _____
_____        _____

**Business**                    **Contact/Customer Service**
_____        _____

**Web Address**
_____

**Log in/username**      **Password**
_____  _____   _____  _____  _____
_____  _____   _____  _____  _____
_____  _____   _____  _____  _____
_____  _____   _____  _____  _____

**Security Question**            **Answer**
_____        _____
_____        _____
_____        _____
_____        _____

**U**

**Business**

**Contact/Customer Service**

**Web Address**

**Log in/username**       **Password**

**Security Question**              **Answer**

**Business**

**Contact/Customer Service**

**Web Address**

**Log in/username**       **Password**

U

**Security Question**              **Answer**

**Business**  _____  **Contact/Customer Service**  _____

**Web Address**  _____

**Log in/username**  _____  **Password**  _____

_____  _____  _____  _____  _____

_____  _____  _____  _____  _____

_____  _____  _____  _____  _____

_____  _____  _____  _____  _____

**Security Question**  _____  **Answer**  _____

_____  _____

_____  _____

_____  _____

_____  _____

**Business**  _____  **Contact/Customer Service**  _____

**Web Address**  _____

**Log in/username**  _____  **Password**  _____

_____  _____  _____  _____  _____

_____  _____  _____  _____  _____

_____  _____  _____  _____  _____

_____  _____  _____  _____  _____

**Security Question**  _____  **Answer**  _____

_____  _____

_____  _____

_____  _____

_____  _____

**U**

**Business**                                    **Contact/Customer Service**

_____          _____

**Web Address**

_____

**Log in/username**        **Password**

_____     _____     _____     _____     _____
_____     _____     _____     _____     _____
_____     _____     _____     _____     _____
_____     _____     _____     _____     _____

**Security Question**                       **Answer**

_____          _____
_____          _____
_____          _____
_____          _____

**Business**                                    **Contact/Customer Service**

_____          _____

**Web Address**

_____

**Log in/username**        **Password**

_____     _____     _____     _____     _____
_____     _____     _____     _____     _____
_____     _____     _____     _____     _____
_____     _____     _____     _____     _____

**V**

**Security Question**                       **Answer**

_____          _____
_____          _____
_____          _____
_____          _____

**Business**

**Contact/Customer Service**

**Web Address**

**Log in/username**          **Password**

**Security Question**

**Answer**

**Business**

**Contact/Customer Service**

**Web Address**

**Log in/username**          **Password**

**Security Question**

**Answer**

V

**Business**           **Contact/Customer Service**

_____  _____

**Web Address**

_____

**Log in/username**    **Password**

_____  _____  _____  _____  _____
_____  _____  _____  _____  _____
_____  _____  _____  _____  _____
_____  _____  _____  _____  _____

**Security Question**       **Answer**

_____  _____
_____  _____
_____  _____
_____  _____

**Business**           **Contact/Customer Service**

_____  _____

**Web Address**

_____

**Log in/username**    **Password**

_____  _____  _____  _____  _____
_____  _____  _____  _____  _____
_____  _____  _____  _____  _____
_____  _____  _____  _____  _____

**V**

**Security Question**       **Answer**

_____  _____
_____  _____
_____  _____
_____  _____

**Business** _____ **Contact/Customer Service**

_____ _____

**Web Address**

_____

**Log in/username** **Password**

_____ _____ _____ _____ _____
_____ _____ _____ _____ _____
_____ _____ _____ _____ _____
_____ _____ _____ _____ _____

**Security Question** **Answer**

_____ _____
_____ _____
_____ _____
_____ _____

**Business** _____ **Contact/Customer Service**

_____ _____

**Web Address**

_____

**Log in/username** **Password**

_____ _____ _____ _____ _____
_____ _____ _____ _____ _____
_____ _____ _____ _____ _____
_____ _____ _____ _____ _____

**Security Question** **Answer**

_____ _____
_____ _____
_____ _____
_____ _____

**V**

**Business**                         **Contact/Customer Service**

_____     _____

**Web Address**

_____

**Log in/username**      **Password**

_____  _____  _____  _____  _____

_____  _____  _____  _____  _____

_____  _____  _____  _____  _____

_____  _____  _____  _____  _____

**Security Question**               **Answer**

_____     _____

_____     _____

_____     _____

_____     _____

---

**Business**                         **Contact/Customer Service**

_____     _____

**Web Address**

_____

**Log in/username**      **Password**

_____  _____  _____  _____  _____

_____  _____  _____  _____  _____

_____  _____  _____  _____  _____

_____  _____  _____  _____  _____

**W**    **Security Question**              **Answer**

_____     _____

_____     _____

_____     _____

_____     _____

**Business** _____ **Contact/Customer Service** _____

**Web Address** _____

**Log in/username** _____ **Password** _____

_____ _____ _____ _____ _____

_____ _____ _____ _____ _____

_____ _____ _____ _____ _____

**Security Question** _____ **Answer** _____

_____ _____

_____ _____

_____ _____

**Business** _____ **Contact/Customer Service** _____

**Web Address** _____

**Log in/username** _____ **Password** _____

_____ _____ _____ _____ _____

_____ _____ _____ _____ _____

_____ _____ _____ _____ _____

_____ _____ _____ _____ _____

**Security Question** _____ **Answer** _____

_____ _____

_____ _____

_____ _____

_____ _____

**W**

**Business**  **Contact/Customer Service**

_____  _____

**Web Address**

_____

**Log in/username**  **Password**

_____  _____  _____  _____  _____
_____  _____  _____  _____  _____
_____  _____  _____  _____  _____
_____  _____  _____  _____  _____

**Security Question**  **Answer**

_____  _____
_____  _____
_____  _____
_____  _____

**Business**  **Contact/Customer Service**

_____  _____

**Web Address**

_____

**Log in/username**  **Password**

_____  _____  _____  _____  _____
_____  _____  _____  _____  _____
_____  _____  _____  _____  _____
_____  _____  _____  _____  _____

**W** **Security Question**  **Answer**

_____  _____
_____  _____
_____  _____
_____  _____

**Business**　　　　　　　　　**Contact/Customer Service**

_____　　_____

**Web Address**

_____

**Log in/username**　　　**Password**

_____　_____　_____　_____　_____

_____　_____　_____　_____　_____

_____　_____　_____　_____　_____

_____　_____　_____　_____　_____

**Security Question**　　　　　**Answer**

_____　　　　_____

_____　　　　_____

_____　　　　_____

_____　　　　_____

**Business**　　　　　　　　　**Contact/Customer Service**

_____　　_____

**Web Address**

_____

**Log in/username**　　　**Password**

_____　_____　_____　_____　_____

_____　_____　_____　_____　_____

_____　_____　_____　_____　_____

_____　_____　_____　_____　_____

**Security Question**　　　　　**Answer**

_____　　　　_____

_____　　　　_____

_____　　　　_____

_____　　　　_____

**W**

**Business**     **Contact/Customer Service**

_____ _____

**Web Address**

_____

**Log in/username**  **Password**

_____  _____  _____  _____  _____
_____  _____  _____  _____  _____
_____  _____  _____  _____  _____
_____  _____  _____  _____  _____

**Security Question**   **Answer**

_____ _____
_____ _____
_____ _____
_____ _____

---

**Business**     **Contact/Customer Service**

_____ _____

**Web Address**

_____

**Log in/username**  **Password**

_____  _____  _____  _____  _____
_____  _____  _____  _____  _____
_____  _____  _____  _____  _____
_____  _____  _____  _____  _____

**Security Question**   **Answer**

_____ _____
_____ _____
_____ _____
_____ _____

X
Y
Z

**Business** _____ **Contact/Customer Service**

_____ _____

**Web Address**

_____

**Log in/username**     **Password**

_____ _____   _____ _____ _____

_____ _____   _____ _____ _____

_____ _____   _____ _____ _____

_____ _____   _____ _____ _____

**Security Question**          **Answer**

_____          _____

_____          _____

_____          _____

_____          _____

---

**Business** _____ **Contact/Customer Service**

_____ _____

**Web Address**

_____

**Log in/username**     **Password**

_____ _____   _____ _____ _____

_____ _____   _____ _____ _____

_____ _____   _____ _____ _____

_____ _____   _____ _____ _____

**Security Question**          **Answer**

_____          _____

_____          _____

_____          _____

_____          _____

**X**
**Y**
**Z**

**Business**                                    **Contact/Customer Service**

_____        _____

**Web Address**

_____

**Log in/username**        **Password**

_____    _____  _____  _____  _____

_____    _____  _____  _____  _____

_____    _____  _____  _____  _____

_____    _____  _____  _____  _____

**Security Question**                           **Answer**

_____        _____

_____        _____

_____        _____

_____        _____

**Business**                                    **Contact/Customer Service**

_____        _____

**Web Address**

_____

**Log in/username**        **Password**

_____    _____  _____  _____  _____

_____    _____  _____  _____  _____

_____    _____  _____  _____  _____

_____    _____  _____  _____  _____

**Security Question**                           **Answer**

_____        _____

_____        _____

_____        _____

_____        _____

**X**
**Y**
**Z**

**Business**                    **Contact/Customer Service**

_____     _____

**Web Address**

_____

**Log in/username**     **Password**

_____  _____     _____  _____  _____

_____  _____     _____  _____  _____

_____  _____     _____  _____  _____

_____  _____     _____  _____  _____

**Security Question**          **Answer**

_____     _____

_____     _____

_____     _____

_____     _____

**Business**                    **Contact/Customer Service**

_____     _____

**Web Address**

_____

**Log in/username**     **Password**

_____  _____     _____  _____  _____

_____  _____     _____  _____  _____

_____  _____     _____  _____  _____

_____  _____     _____  _____  _____

**Security Question**          **Answer**

_____     _____

_____     _____

_____     _____

_____     _____

**X**
**Y**
**Z**

# A

**Name**

**Address**

**email**

**Phone/text**
smart phone/text messaging: _____
Work: _____
Home (LAN): _____
Other (_____): _____

**Name**

**Address**

**email**

**Phone/text**
smart phone/text messaging: _____
Work: _____
Home (LAN): _____
Other (_____): _____

**Friends and Family**

**Name**

**Address**

**email**

**Phone/text**
   smart phone/text messaging: _____
                    Work: _____
            Home (LAN): _____
   Other (_____): _____

**Name**

**Address**

**email**

**Phone/text**
   smart phone/text messaging: _____
                    Work: _____
            Home (LAN): _____
   Other (_____): _____

**Friends and Family**

# A

**Name**

**Address**

**email**

**Phone/text**

smart phone/text messaging: _____

Work: _____

Home (LAN): _____

Other (_____): _____

**Name**

**Address**

**email**

**Phone/text**

smart phone/text messaging: _____

Work: _____

Home (LAN): _____

Other (_____): _____

**Friends and Family**

**Name**

**Address**

**email**

**Phone/text**
   smart phone/text messaging: _____
                 Work: _____
          Home (LAN): _____
   Other (_____): _____

**Name**

**Address**

**email**

**Phone/text**
   smart phone/text messaging: _____
                 Work: _____
          Home (LAN): _____
   Other (_____): _____

**Friends and Family**

**B**

Name
_____

Address
_____

_____    _____
_____    _____
_____    _____
_____    _____

email

_____
_____
_____
_____

Phone/text
  smart phone/text messaging:  _____
                      Work:  _____
                Home (LAN):  _____
  Other (_____):  _____

Name
_____

Address
_____

_____    _____
_____    _____
_____    _____
_____    _____

email

_____
_____
_____
_____

Phone/text
  smart phone/text messaging:  _____
                      Work:  _____
                Home (LAN):  _____
  Other (_____):  _____

**Friends and Family**

**Name** _____

**Address** _____

_____     _____
_____     _____
_____     _____
_____     _____

**email**

_____
_____
_____
_____

**Phone/text**
smart phone/text messaging:  _____
Work:  _____
Home (LAN):  _____
Other (_____):  _____

**Name** _____

**Address** _____

_____     _____
_____     _____
_____     _____
_____     _____

**email**

_____
_____
_____
_____

**Phone/text**
smart phone/text messaging:  _____
Work:  _____
Home (LAN):  _____
Other (_____):  _____

**Friends and Family**

**B**

**Name**

**Address**

**email**

**Phone/text**
smart phone/text messaging: _____
Work: _____
Home (LAN): _____
Other (_____): _____

**Name**

**Address**

**email**

**Phone/text**
smart phone/text messaging: _____
Work: _____
Home (LAN): _____
Other (_____): _____

**Friends and Family**

**Name**

**Address**

**email**

**Phone/text**
    smart phone/text messaging: _____
                      Work: _____
            Home (LAN): _____
    Other (_____): _____

**Name**

**Address**

**email**

**Phone/text**
    smart phone/text messaging: _____
                      Work: _____
            Home (LAN): _____
    Other (_____): _____

**Friends and Family**

Name

**Address**

email

**Phone/text**
smart phone/text messaging: _____
Work: _____
Home (LAN): _____
Other (_____): _____

Name

**Address**

email

**Phone/text**
smart phone/text messaging: _____
Work: _____
Home (LAN): _____
Other (_____): _____

**C**

**Friends and Family**

**Name**

**Address**

**email**

**Phone/text**
smart phone/text messaging: _____
Work: _____
Home (LAN): _____
Other (_____): _____

**Name**

**Address**

**email**

**Phone/text**
smart phone/text messaging: _____
Work: _____
Home (LAN): _____
Other (_____): _____

**Name**

**Address**

**email**

**Phone/text**
smart phone/text messaging: _____
Work: _____
Home (LAN): _____
Other (_____): _____

**Name**

**Address**

**email**

**Phone/text**
smart phone/text messaging: _____
Work: _____
Home (LAN): _____
Other (_____): _____

**Friends and Family**

**Name**

**Address**

**email**

**Phone/text**
   smart phone/text messaging: _____
                   Work: _____
          Home (LAN): _____
  Other (_____): _____

**Name**

**Address**

**email**

**Phone/text**
   smart phone/text messaging: _____
                   Work: _____
          Home (LAN): _____
  Other (_____): _____

**Friends and Family**

**D**

**Friends and Family**

Name

Address

_____     _____
_____     _____
_____     _____
_____     _____

email

_____
_____
_____
_____

Phone/text
   smart phone/text messaging: _____
                    Work: _____
             Home (LAN): _____
  Other (_____): _____

Name

Address

_____     _____
_____     _____
_____     _____
_____     _____

email

_____
_____
_____
_____

Phone/text
   smart phone/text messaging: _____
                    Work: _____
             Home (LAN): _____
  Other (_____): _____

**Name**

**Address**

**email**

**Phone/text**
  smart phone/text messaging: _____
                    Work: _____
           Home (LAN): _____
  Other (_____): _____

**Name**

**Address**

**email**

**Phone/text**
  smart phone/text messaging: _____
                    Work: _____
           Home (LAN): _____
  Other (_____): _____

**Friends and Family**

**Name**

**Address**

**D**

**email**

**Phone/text**
 smart phone/text messaging: _____
        Work: _____
      Home (LAN): _____
 Other (_____): _____

**Name**

**Address**

**email**

**Phone/text**
 smart phone/text messaging: _____
        Work: _____
      Home (LAN): _____
 Other (_____): _____

**Friends and Family**

**Name**

**Address**

**email**

**Phone/text**
   smart phone/text messaging:
                            Work:
                 Home (LAN):
   Other (_____):

**Name**

**Address**

**email**

**Phone/text**
   smart phone/text messaging:
                            Work:
                 Home (LAN):
   Other (_____):

**Friends and Family**

**Name**

**Address**

**email**

**Phone/text**
smart phone/text messaging: _____
Work: _____
Home (LAN): _____
Other (_____): _____

**Name**

**Address**

**email**

**Phone/text**
smart phone/text messaging: _____
Work: _____
Home (LAN): _____
Other (_____): _____

**Name**

**Address**

**email**

**Phone/text**
   smart phone/text messaging:
                        Work:
               Home (LAN):
  Other (_____):

**Name**

**Address**

**email**

**Phone/text**
   smart phone/text messaging:
                        Work:
               Home (LAN):
  Other (_____):

**E**

**Friends and Family**

**Name**

**Address**

**email**

**Phone/text**
smart phone/text messaging:
Work:
Home (LAN):
Other (_____):

**Name**

**Address**

**email**

**Phone/text**
smart phone/text messaging:
Work:
Home (LAN):
Other (_____):

**Name**

**Address**

email

**Phone/text**
   smart phone/text messaging: _____
                     Work: _____
           Home (LAN): _____
   Other (_____): _____

**Name**

**Address**

email

**Phone/text**
   smart phone/text messaging: _____
                     Work: _____
           Home (LAN): _____
   Other (_____): _____

**Name**

**Address**

**F**

**email**

**Phone/text**
smart phone/text messaging:
Work:
Home (LAN):
Other (_____):

**Name**

**Address**

**email**

**Phone/text**
smart phone/text messaging:
Work:
Home (LAN):
Other (_____):

**Friends and Family**

**Name**

**Address**

**email**

**Phone/text**
smart phone/text messaging: _____
Work: _____
Home (LAN): _____
Other (_____): _____

**Name**

**Address**

**email**

**Phone/text**
smart phone/text messaging: _____
Work: _____
Home (LAN): _____
Other (_____): _____

**Name**

**Address**

**email**

**Phone/text**
  smart phone/text messaging:
                        Work:
                   Home (LAN):
  Other (_____):

**Name**

**Address**

**email**

**Phone/text**
  smart phone/text messaging:
                        Work:
                   Home (LAN):
  Other (_____):

**Name**

**Address**

**email**

**Phone/text**
smart phone/text messaging:
Work:
Home (LAN):
Other (_____):

**Name**

**Address**

**email**

**Phone/text**
smart phone/text messaging:
Work:
Home (LAN):
Other (_____):

**Name**

**Address**

**email**

**Phone/text**
   smart phone/text messaging: _____
                  Work: _____
          Home (LAN): _____
  Other (_____): _____

**Name**

**Address**

**email**

**Phone/text**
   smart phone/text messaging: _____
                  Work: _____
          Home (LAN): _____
  Other (_____): _____

**Name**

**Address**

email

**Phone/text**
 smart phone/text messaging: _____
 Work: _____
 Home (LAN): _____
 Other (_____): _____

**Name**

**Address**

email

**Phone/text**
 smart phone/text messaging: _____
 Work: _____
 Home (LAN): _____
 Other (_____): _____

**Friends and Family**

**Name**

**Address**

**G**

email

**Phone/text**
smart phone/text messaging: _____
Work: _____
Home (LAN): _____
Other (_____): _____

**Name**

**Address**

email

**Phone/text**
smart phone/text messaging: _____
Work: _____
Home (LAN): _____
Other (_____): _____

**Friends and Family**

**Name**

**Address**

_____    _____
_____    _____
_____    _____
_____    _____

**email**

_____
_____
_____
_____

**Phone/text**
smart phone/text messaging: _____
Work: _____
Home (LAN): _____
Other (_____): _____

**Name**

**Address**

_____    _____
_____    _____
_____    _____
_____    _____

**email**

_____
_____
_____
_____

**Phone/text**
smart phone/text messaging: _____
Work: _____
Home (LAN): _____
Other (_____): _____

**Friends and Family**

Name

Address

email

Phone/text
    smart phone/text messaging:
                        Work:
                  Home (LAN):
    Other (_____):

Name

Address

email

Phone/text
    smart phone/text messaging:
                        Work:
                  Home (LAN):
    Other (_____):

**Friends and Family**

126

**Name**

**Address**

email

**Phone/text**
   smart phone/text messaging: _____
                        Work: _____
                  Home (LAN): _____
   Other (_____): _____

**Name**

**Address**

email

**Phone/text**
   smart phone/text messaging: _____
                        Work: _____
                  Home (LAN): _____
   Other (_____): _____

**Name**

**Address**

email

**Phone/text**
smart phone/text messaging: _____
Work: _____
Home (LAN): _____
Other (_____): _____

**Name**

**Address**

email

**Phone/text**
smart phone/text messaging: _____
Work: _____
Home (LAN): _____
Other (_____): _____

**Name**

**Address**

**email**

H

**Phone/text**
  smart phone/text messaging: _____
                        Work: _____
                  Home (LAN): _____
  Other (_____): _____

**Name**

**Address**

**email**

**Phone/text**
  smart phone/text messaging: _____
                        Work: _____
                  Home (LAN): _____
  Other (_____): _____

**Friends and Family**

**Name**

**Address**

**email**

**Phone/text**
smart phone/text messaging: _____
Work: _____
Home (LAN): _____
Other (_____): _____

**Name**

**Address**

**email**

**Phone/text**
smart phone/text messaging: _____
Work: _____
Home (LAN): _____
Other (_____): _____

**Friends and Family**

**Name**

**Address**

**email**

**Phone/text**
smart phone/text messaging: _____
Work: _____
Home (LAN): _____
Other (_____): _____

**Name**

**Address**

**email**

**Phone/text**
smart phone/text messaging: _____
Work: _____
Home (LAN): _____
Other (_____): _____

**Friends and Family**

**Name**

**Address**

_____    _____
_____    _____
_____    _____
_____    _____

**email**

_____
_____
_____
_____

**Phone/text**
   smart phone/text messaging: _____
                       Work: _____
            Home (LAN): _____
  Other (_____): _____

**Name**

**Address**

_____    _____
_____    _____
_____    _____
_____    _____

**email**

_____
_____
_____
_____

**Phone/text**
   smart phone/text messaging: _____
                       Work: _____
            Home (LAN): _____
  Other (_____): _____

**Friends and Family**

**Name**

**Address**

_____

_____

_____

_____

**email**

**Phone/text**
  smart phone/text messaging: _____
                      Work: _____
               Home (LAN): _____
  Other (_____): _____

**Name**

**Address**

_____

_____

_____

**email**

**Phone/text**
  smart phone/text messaging: _____
                      Work: _____
               Home (LAN): _____
  Other (_____): _____

**Friends and Family**

**Name**

**Address**

**email**

**Phone/text**
smart phone/text messaging: _____
Work: _____
Home (LAN): _____
Other (_____): _____

**Name**

**Address**

**email**

**Phone/text**
smart phone/text messaging: _____
Work: _____
Home (LAN): _____
Other (_____): _____

**Friends and Family**

**Name**

**Address**

**email**

**Phone/text**
  smart phone/text messaging: _____
                        Work: _____
                  Home (LAN): _____
    Other (_____): _____

**Name**

**Address**

**email**

**Phone/text**
  smart phone/text messaging: _____
                        Work: _____
                  Home (LAN): _____
    Other (_____): _____

**Name**

**Address**

_____     _____
_____     _____
_____     _____
_____     _____

**email**

_____
_____
_____
_____

**Phone/text**
   smart phone/text messaging: _____
                 Work: _____
          Home (LAN): _____
   Other (_____): _____

**Name**

**Address**

_____     _____
_____     _____
_____     _____
_____     _____

**email**

_____
_____
_____
_____

**Phone/text**
   smart phone/text messaging: _____
                 Work: _____
          Home (LAN): _____
   Other (_____): _____

**Friends and Family**

**Name**

**Address**

_____  _____
_____  _____
_____  _____
_____  _____

**email**

_____
_____
_____
_____

**Phone/text**
smart phone/text messaging: _____
Work: _____
Home (LAN): _____
Other (_____): _____

**Name**

**Address**

_____  _____
_____  _____
_____  _____
_____  _____

**email**

_____
_____
_____
_____

**Phone/text**
smart phone/text messaging: _____
Work: _____
Home (LAN): _____
Other (_____): _____

**Friends and Family**

**Name**

**Address**

**email**

**K**

**Phone/text**
    smart phone/text messaging: _____
                        Work: _____
                Home (LAN): _____
    Other (_____): _____

**Name**

**Address**

**email**

**Phone/text**
    smart phone/text messaging: _____
                        Work: _____
                Home (LAN): _____
    Other (_____): _____

**Friends and Family**

**Name**
_____

**Address**

_____  _____
_____  _____
_____  _____
_____  _____

**email**

_____
_____
_____
_____

**Phone/text**
   smart phone/text messaging:  _____
                        Work:  _____
                  Home (LAN):  _____
   Other (_____):  _____

**Name**
_____

**Address**

_____  _____
_____  _____
_____  _____
_____  _____

**email**

_____
_____
_____
_____

**Phone/text**
   smart phone/text messaging:  _____
                        Work:  _____
                  Home (LAN):  _____
   Other (_____):  _____

K

Friends and Family

**Name**

**Address**

email

**Phone/text**
　　smart phone/text messaging:
　　　　　　　　　　　Work:
　　　　　　　　Home (LAN):
　　Other (_____):

**Name**

**Address**

email

**Phone/text**
　　smart phone/text messaging:
　　　　　　　　　　　Work:
　　　　　　　　Home (LAN):
　　Other (_____):

**Friends and Family**

**Name**

**Address**

**email**

**Phone/text**
smart phone/text messaging: _____
Work: _____
Home (LAN): _____
Other (_____): _____

**K**

**Name**

**Address**

**email**

**Phone/text**
smart phone/text messaging: _____
Work: _____
Home (LAN): _____
Other (_____): _____

**Friends and Family**

**Name**

**Address**

**email**

**Phone/text**
smart phone/text messaging: _____
Work: _____
Home (LAN): _____
Other (_____): _____

**Name**

**Address**

**email**

**Phone/text**
smart phone/text messaging: _____
Work: _____
Home (LAN): _____
Other (_____): _____

**L**

**Friends and Family**

**Name**

**Address**

**email**

**Phone/text**
smart phone/text messaging: _____
Work: _____
Home (LAN): _____
Other (_____): _____

**Name**

**Address**

**email**

**Phone/text**
smart phone/text messaging: _____
Work: _____
Home (LAN): _____
Other (_____): _____

**L**

**Friends and Family**

**Name**

**Address**

**email**

**Phone/text**
smart phone/text messaging: _____
Work: _____
Home (LAN): _____
Other (_____): _____

**L**

**Name**

**Address**

**email**

**Phone/text**
smart phone/text messaging: _____
Work: _____
Home (LAN): _____
Other (_____): _____

**Friends and Family**

**Name**

**Address**

**email**

**Phone/text**
   smart phone/text messaging: _____
                    Work: _____
             Home (LAN): _____
   Other (_____): _____

**Name**

**Address**

**email**

**Phone/text**
   smart phone/text messaging: _____
                    Work: _____
             Home (LAN): _____
   Other (_____): _____

L

**Friends and Family**

**Name**

**Address**

**email**

**Phone/text**
smart phone/text messaging: _____
Work: _____
Home (LAN): _____
Other (_____): _____

**Name**

**Address**

**email**

**Phone/text**
smart phone/text messaging: _____
Work: _____
Home (LAN): _____
Other (_____): _____

**M**

**Friends and Family**

**Name**

**Address**

**email**

**Phone/text**
   smart phone/text messaging: _____
                      Work: _____
            Home (LAN): _____
   Other (_____): _____

**M**

**Name**

**Address**

**email**

**Phone/text**
   smart phone/text messaging: _____
                      Work: _____
            Home (LAN): _____
   Other (_____): _____

**Friends and Family**

**Name**

**Address**

**email**

**Phone/text**
smart phone/text messaging: _____
Work: _____
Home (LAN): _____
Other (_____): _____

**M**

**Name**

**Address**

**email**

**Phone/text**
smart phone/text messaging: _____
Work: _____
Home (LAN): _____
Other (_____): _____

**Friends and Family**

**Name**

**Address**

_____     _____
_____     _____
_____     _____
_____     _____

**email**

_____
_____
_____
_____

**Phone/text**
   smart phone/text messaging: _____
                    Work: _____
           Home (LAN): _____
  Other (_____): _____

**M**

**Name**

**Address**

_____     _____
_____     _____
_____     _____
_____     _____

**email**

_____
_____
_____
_____

**Phone/text**
   smart phone/text messaging: _____
                    Work: _____
           Home (LAN): _____
  Other (_____): _____

**Friends and Family**

**N**

**Name**

**Address**

**email**

**Phone/text**
smart phone/text messaging: _____
Work: _____
Home (LAN): _____
Other (_____): _____

**Name**

**Address**

**email**

**Phone/text**
smart phone/text messaging: _____
Work: _____
Home (LAN): _____
Other (_____): _____

Name _____

Address _____

_____      _____
_____      _____
_____      _____
_____      _____

email

_____
_____
_____
_____

Phone/text
  smart phone/text messaging: _____
                  Work: _____
           Home (LAN): _____
  Other (_____): _____

Name _____

Address _____

_____      _____
_____      _____
_____      _____
_____      _____

email

_____
_____
_____
_____

Phone/text
  smart phone/text messaging: _____
                  Work: _____
           Home (LAN): _____
  Other (_____): _____

**N**

**Name**

**Address**

**email**

**Phone/text**
    smart phone/text messaging: _____
                         Work: _____
                  Home (LAN): _____
        Other (_____): _____

**Name**

**Address**

**email**

**Phone/text**
    smart phone/text messaging: _____
                         Work: _____
                  Home (LAN): _____
        Other (_____): _____

**Name**
_____

**Address**
_____     _____
_____     _____
_____     _____
_____     _____

**email**

_____
_____
_____
_____

**Phone/text**
  smart phone/text messaging: _____
                     Work: _____
           Home (LAN): _____
   Other (_____): _____

**Name**
_____

**Address**
_____     _____
_____     _____
_____     _____

**email**

_____
_____
_____
_____

**Phone/text**
  smart phone/text messaging: _____
                     Work: _____
           Home (LAN): _____
   Other (_____): _____

**Friends and Family**

Name

Address

email

Phone/text
    smart phone/text messaging:
                          Work:
                 Home (LAN):
    Other (_____):

Name

Address

email

Phone/text
    smart phone/text messaging:
                          Work:
                 Home (LAN):
    Other (_____):

O

**Name**

_____

**Address**

_____        _____
_____        _____
_____        _____
_____        _____

**email**

_____
_____
_____
_____

**Phone/text**
   smart phone/text messaging: _____
                     Work: _____
            Home (LAN): _____
  Other (_____): _____

**Name**

_____

**O**

**Address**

_____        _____
_____        _____
_____        _____
_____        _____

**email**

_____
_____
_____
_____

**Phone/text**
   smart phone/text messaging: _____
                     Work: _____
            Home (LAN): _____
  Other (_____): _____

Name

Address

email

Phone/text
smart phone/text messaging:
Work:
Home (LAN):
Other (_____):

O

Name

Address

email

Phone/text
smart phone/text messaging:
Work:
Home (LAN):
Other (_____):

**Name**
_____

**Address**
_____     _____
_____     _____
_____     _____
_____     _____

**email**
_____
_____
_____
_____

**Phone/text**
   smart phone/text messaging:   _____
                     Work:   _____
           Home (LAN):   _____
   Other (_____):   _____

**O**

**Name**
_____

**Address**
_____     _____
_____     _____
_____     _____

**email**
_____
_____
_____
_____

**Phone/text**
   smart phone/text messaging:   _____
                     Work:   _____
           Home (LAN):   _____
   Other (_____):   _____

Name

Address

email

Phone/text
smart phone/text messaging: _____
Work: _____
Home (LAN): _____
Other (_____): _____

**P**

Name

Address

email

Phone/text
smart phone/text messaging: _____
Work: _____
Home (LAN): _____
Other (_____): _____

Name _____

Address _____

_____    _____
_____    _____
_____    _____
_____    _____

email

_____
_____
_____
_____

Phone/text
   smart phone/text messaging: _____
                Work: _____
          Home (LAN): _____
   Other (_____): _____

Name _____

Address _____

_____    _____
_____    _____
_____    _____
_____    _____

email

_____
_____
_____
_____

Phone/text
   smart phone/text messaging: _____
                Work: _____
          Home (LAN): _____
   Other (_____): _____

**Name**

**Address**

**email**

**Phone/text**

    smart phone/text messaging: _____

                       Work: _____

               Home (LAN): _____

    Other (_____): _____

**P**

**Name**

**Address**

**email**

**Phone/text**

    smart phone/text messaging: _____

                       Work: _____

               Home (LAN): _____

    Other (_____): _____

Name

Address

_____    _____
_____    _____
_____    _____
_____    _____

email

_____
_____
_____
_____

Phone/text
  smart phone/text messaging: _____
                  Work: _____
           Home (LAN): _____
  Other (_____): _____

Name

Address

**P**

_____    _____
_____    _____
_____    _____
_____    _____

email

_____
_____
_____
_____

Phone/text
  smart phone/text messaging: _____
                  Work: _____
           Home (LAN): _____
  Other (_____): _____

**Name**

**Address**

**email**

**Phone/text**
    smart phone/text messaging: _____
                      Work: _____
             Home (LAN): _____
    Other (_____): _____

**Q**

**Name**

**Address**

**email**

**Phone/text**
    smart phone/text messaging: _____
                      Work: _____
             Home (LAN): _____
    Other (_____): _____

**Name**

**Address**

**email**

**Phone/text**
   smart phone/text messaging: _____
                   Work: _____
           Home (LAN): _____
  Other (_____): _____

**Name**

**Address**

**email**

**Phone/text**
   smart phone/text messaging: _____
                   Work: _____
           Home (LAN): _____
  Other (_____): _____

**Q**

Name

Address

email

Phone/text
   smart phone/text messaging: _____
                     Work: _____
             Home (LAN): _____
   Other (_____): _____

Name

Address

**Q**

email

Phone/text
   smart phone/text messaging: _____
                     Work: _____
             Home (LAN): _____
   Other (_____): _____

**Name**

**Address**

**email**

**Phone/text**
    smart phone/text messaging:
                     Work:
            Home (LAN):
    Other (_____):

**Q**

**Name**

**Address**

**email**

**Phone/text**
    smart phone/text messaging:
                     Work:
            Home (LAN):
    Other (_____):

**Friends and Family**

**R**

Name

Address

email

Phone/text
smart phone/text messaging: _____
Work: _____
Home (LAN): _____
Other (_____): _____

Name

Address

email

Phone/text
smart phone/text messaging: _____
Work: _____
Home (LAN): _____
Other (_____): _____

**Name**

**Address**

**email**

**Phone/text**
 smart phone/text messaging: _____
                        Work: _____
                 Home (LAN): _____
 Other (_____): _____

**Name**

**Address**

R

**email**

**Phone/text**
 smart phone/text messaging: _____
                        Work: _____
                 Home (LAN): _____
 Other (_____): _____

**Name**

**Address**

_____    _____
_____    _____
_____    _____

**email**

_____
_____
_____
_____

**Phone/text**
    smart phone/text messaging: _____
                 Work: _____
          Home (LAN): _____
    Other (_____): _____

**R**

**Name**

**Address**

_____    _____
_____    _____
_____    _____

**email**

_____
_____
_____
_____

**Phone/text**
    smart phone/text messaging: _____
                 Work: _____
          Home (LAN): _____
    Other (_____): _____

**Name**

**Address**

**email**

**Phone/text**
smart phone/text messaging: _____
Work: _____
Home (LAN): _____
Other (_____): _____

**Name**

**Address**

R

**email**

**Phone/text**
smart phone/text messaging: _____
Work: _____
Home (LAN): _____
Other (_____): _____

**Name**

**Address**

email

**Phone/text**
smart phone/text messaging: _____
Work: _____
Home (LAN): _____
Other (_____): _____

**Name**

**Address**

S

email

**Phone/text**
smart phone/text messaging: _____
Work: _____
Home (LAN): _____
Other (_____): _____

Name
_____

Address
_____    _____
_____    _____
_____    _____

email
_____
_____
_____
_____

Phone/text
smart phone/text messaging: _____
Work: _____
Home (LAN): _____
Other (_____): _____

Name
_____

Address
_____    _____
_____    _____
_____    _____

**S**

email
_____
_____
_____
_____

Phone/text
smart phone/text messaging: _____
Work: _____
Home (LAN): _____
Other (_____): _____

**Friends and Family**

Name

Address

email

Phone/text
smart phone/text messaging:
Work:
Home (LAN):
Other (_____):

Name

Address

**S**

email

Phone/text
smart phone/text messaging:
Work:
Home (LAN):
Other (_____):

**Name** _____

**Address** _____

_____ _____
_____ _____
_____ _____
_____ _____

**email**

_____
_____
_____
_____

**Phone/text**
smart phone/text messaging: _____
Work: _____
Home (LAN): _____
Other (_____): _____

**Name** _____

**Address** _____

_____ _____
_____ _____
_____ _____
_____ _____

**S**

**email**

_____
_____
_____
_____

**Phone/text**
smart phone/text messaging: _____
Work: _____
Home (LAN): _____
Other (_____): _____

**Name**

**Address**

**email**

**Phone/text**
smart phone/text messaging: _____
Work: _____
Home (LAN): _____
Other (_____): _____

**Name**

**Address**

T

**email**

**Phone/text**
smart phone/text messaging: _____
Work: _____
Home (LAN): _____
Other (_____): _____

**Name**

_____

**Address**

_____    _____
_____    _____
_____    _____
_____    _____

**email**

_____
_____
_____
_____

**Phone/text**
   smart phone/text messaging:  _____
                         **Work:**  _____
             **Home (LAN):**  _____
   **Other (_____):**  _____

**Name**

_____

**Address**

_____    _____
_____    _____
_____    _____
_____    _____

**email**

_____
_____
_____
_____

**Phone/text**
   smart phone/text messaging:  _____
                         **Work:**  _____
             **Home (LAN):**  _____
   **Other (_____):**  _____

**T**

Name
_____

Address
_____

_____     _____
_____     _____
_____     _____
_____     _____

email
_____
_____
_____
_____

Phone/text
  smart phone/text messaging: _____
                     Work: _____
           Home (LAN): _____
  Other (_____): _____

Name
_____

Address
_____

_____     _____
_____     _____
_____     _____
_____     _____

T

email
_____
_____
_____
_____

Phone/text
  smart phone/text messaging: _____
                     Work: _____
           Home (LAN): _____
  Other (_____): _____

**Name**

**Address**

**email**

**Phone/text**
    smart phone/text messaging:
                    Work:
             Home (LAN):
    Other (_____):

**Name**

**Address**

**email**

T

**Phone/text**
    smart phone/text messaging:
                    Work:
             Home (LAN):
    Other (_____):

**Friends and Family**

Name

Address

email

Phone/text

smart phone/text messaging:

Work:

Home (LAN):

Other (_____):

Name

Address

email

**U**

Phone/text

smart phone/text messaging:

Work:

Home (LAN):

Other (_____):

**Name**

**Address**

**email**

**Phone/text**
smart phone/text messaging: _____
Work: _____
Home (LAN): _____
Other (_____): _____

**Name**

**Address**

**email**

**Phone/text**
smart phone/text messaging: _____
Work: _____
Home (LAN): _____
Other (_____): _____

U

**Name**

**Address**

**email**

**Phone/text**
smart phone/text messaging:
Work:
Home (LAN):
Other (_____):

**Name**

**Address**

**email**

**U**

**Phone/text**
smart phone/text messaging:
Work:
Home (LAN):
Other (_____):

Name
_____

Address
_____    _____
_____    _____
_____    _____
_____    _____

email
_____
_____
_____
_____

Phone/text
   smart phone/text messaging: _____
                           Work: _____
              Home (LAN): _____
   Other (_____): _____

Name
_____

Address
_____    _____
_____    _____
_____    _____
_____    _____

email
_____
_____
_____
_____

Phone/text
   smart phone/text messaging: _____
                           Work: _____
              Home (LAN): _____
   Other (_____): _____

**U**

Name

Address

email

Phone/text
 smart phone/text messaging: _____
       Work: _____
     Home (LAN): _____
 Other (_____): _____

Name

Address

email

**V**

Phone/text
 smart phone/text messaging: _____
       Work: _____
     Home (LAN): _____
 Other (_____): _____

**Name**
_____

**Address**
_____    _____
_____    _____
_____    _____
_____    _____

**email**
_____
_____
_____
_____

**Phone/text**
　　smart phone/text messaging: _____
　　　　　　　　　　Work: _____
　　　　　　　Home (LAN): _____
　　Other (_____): _____

**Name**
_____

**Address**
_____    _____
_____    _____
_____    _____

**email**
_____
_____
_____
_____

**V**

**Phone/text**
　　smart phone/text messaging: _____
　　　　　　　　　　Work: _____
　　　　　　　Home (LAN): _____
　　Other (_____): _____

**V**

Name

Address

email

Phone/text
smart phone/text messaging: _____
Work: _____
Home (LAN): _____
Other (_____): _____

Name

Address

email

Phone/text
smart phone/text messaging: _____
Work: _____
Home (LAN): _____
Other (_____): _____

Name

Address

_____    _____

email

_____

Phone/text
    smart phone/text messaging: _____
                        Work: _____
                 Home (LAN): _____
    Other (_____): _____

Name

Address

_____    _____

email

_____

**V**

Phone/text
    smart phone/text messaging: _____
                        Work: _____
                 Home (LAN): _____
    Other (_____): _____

**Name**

**Address**

**email**

**Phone/text**
   smart phone/text messaging:
                       Work:
             Home (LAN):
    Other (_____):

**Name**

**Address**

**email**

**W**

**Phone/text**
   smart phone/text messaging:
                       Work:
             Home (LAN):
    Other (_____):

**Name**

**Address**

**email**

**Phone/text**
smart phone/text messaging:
Work:
Home (LAN):
Other (_____):

**Name**

**Address**

**email**

**Phone/text**
smart phone/text messaging:
Work:
Home (LAN):
Other (_____):

**W**

Name

Address

email

Phone/text
smart phone/text messaging: _____
Work: _____
Home (LAN): _____
Other (_____): _____

Name

Address

email

**W**

Phone/text
smart phone/text messaging: _____
Work: _____
Home (LAN): _____
Other (_____): _____

**Name**
_____

**Address**
_____    _____
_____    _____
_____    _____
_____    _____

**email**
_____
_____
_____
_____

**Phone/text**
smart phone/text messaging:  _____
Work:  _____
Home (LAN):  _____
Other (_____):  _____

**Name**
_____

**Address**
_____    _____
_____    _____
_____    _____
_____    _____

**email**
_____
_____
_____
_____

**W**

**Phone/text**
smart phone/text messaging:  _____
Work:  _____
Home (LAN):  _____
Other (_____):  _____

**Name**

**Address**

**email**

**Phone/text**
smart phone/text messaging:
Work:
Home (LAN):
Other (_____):

**Name**

**Address**

**email**

**Phone/text**
smart phone/text messaging:
Work:
Home (LAN):
Other (_____):

**X**
**Y**
**Z**

**Name**

**Address**

**email**

**Phone/text**
  smart phone/text messaging:
                    Work:
          Home (LAN):
  Other (_____):

**Name**

**Address**

**email**

**Phone/text**
  smart phone/text messaging:
                    Work:
          Home (LAN):
  Other (_____):

**X**
**Y**
**Z**

**Name**

**Address**

**email**

**Phone/text**
smart phone/text messaging: _____
Work: _____
Home (LAN): _____
Other (_____): _____

**Name**

**Address**

**email**

**Phone/text**
smart phone/text messaging: _____
Work: _____
Home (LAN): _____
Other (_____): _____

**Name**

**Address**

**email**

**Phone/text**
 smart phone/text messaging: _____
 Work: _____
 Home (LAN): _____
 Other (_____): _____

**Name**

**Address**

**email**

**Phone/text**
 smart phone/text messaging: _____
 Work: _____
 Home (LAN): _____
 Other (_____): _____

CPSIA information can be obtained
at www.ICGtesting.com
Printed in the USA
BVHW051711030223
657843BV00014B/585